NAME ______________________ DATE ________

GRADE ______________________ SCORE ________

AF618829

COLOR MATHEMAGIC

Use addition to blend and create your own colors!

Fill the shapes in column A with colors of your own choosing. Fill the circles in column B with other colors. Mix the paint you used in A and B to create a new color in column C. What new colors did you create?

1.) ◯ + ◯ = ◯

2.) ◯ + ◯ = ◯

3.) ◯ + ◯ = ◯

4.) ◯ + ◯ = ◯

Name: ______________________ Date: ______________________

Days of the week

Trace the letters to spell out the days.

Sunday

Monday

Tuesday

Wednesday

Thursday

Friday

Saturday

Name: Date:
Section: Score:

ADD THE DINOS!

How many dinosaurs are there?

Instructions: How many dinosaurs are there in each line? Add them up and write your answer on the box. When you're done, color them in!

Name:

Date:

Tracing Letters

Practice writing the alphabet by tracing the letters below.

Aa Bb Cc Dd

Ee Ff Gg Hh

Ii Jj Kk Ll

Mm Nn Oo Pp

Qq Rr Ss Tt

Uu Vv Ww Xx

Yy Zz

Name: ______________________ Date: ______________________

Section: ______________________ Score: ______________________

YOU CAN COUNT ON ME!

How many acorns can Mr. Squirrel collect?

Instructions: Count how many acorns there are and write the number on this blank _____.

Letter Sounds

Name:

Class:

Teacher:

Date:

Say the name of each picture out loud and circle the beginning sound.

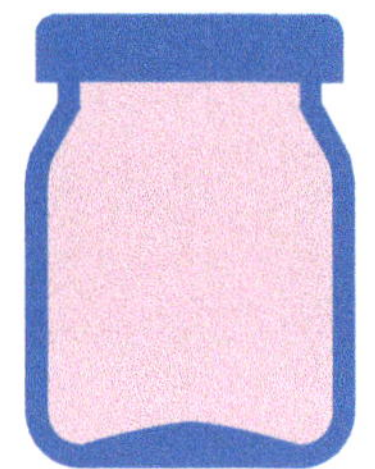

d j

h b

b d

s a

t s

c b

c d

k c

NAME:

SECTION:

DATE:

SCORE:

SNAKES & STRIPES

A COUNTING GAME

Directions: Give this snake its stripes. Draw 3 orange stripes on its neck, 2 green stripes on its body and 5 brown stripes on its tail.

Name: ____________________ Section: ____________________

Teacher: ____________________ Date: ____________________

What letter is next?

Look at the following letters and write down what you think is next in the circle.

D E F ◯	L M N ◯
S T U ◯	P Q R ◯
A B C ◯	H I J ◯
O P Q ◯	V W X ◯

Name: ______________________ Date: ____________

Section: ______________________ Score: ____________

FRUIT MATH

LET'S ADD THESE FRUITS UP!

Directions: How many fruits can you see? Add them all up, then write the answer in the box. Make sure to double check your answers before submitting! Perfect scores get a prize from Ms. Lucy.

Student Name: ______________________ Teacher: ______________________

Class: ______________________ Date: ______________________

The Missing Letter

Look at the pictures below. Say what you see out loud.
What do you hear? Add the missing letter on the blank.

h e _

h a _

_ n t

s _ n

_ w l

t _ p

m u _

Name

Date

Class

Score

Counting Cats and Dogs

AN ADDITION GAME

Directions: Count how many of each animal you see. Write the answers in the box provided below.

Cats [ ]

Dogs [ ]

NAME	TEACHER
CLASS	DATE

LETTER MIX-UP!

Unscramble the letters to spell the words correctly

c k l c o

_ _ _ _ _

o l b e g

_ _ _ _ _

a t p e

_ _ _ _

s o e s h

_ _ _ _ _

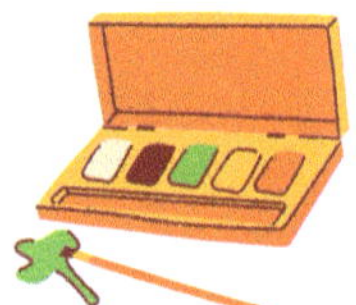

n t a i p

_ _ _ _ _

a l e d m

_ _ _ _ _

p l p e a

_ _ _ _ _

s i p n

_ _ _ _

NAME:

TEACHER:

GRADE & SECTION:

DATE:

KANDI'S CANDY JARS

Kandi won a contest! Help her choose her prize by coloring in the candy jars with more candy in each pairing.

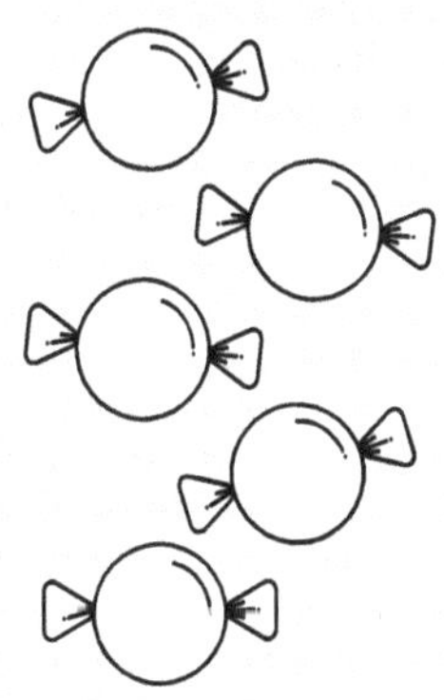

name

date

MY PET SPOT

Read the short story and answer the questions below.

My name is Tommy. I have a dog named Spot. He is small and has brown fur. Spot likes to run around and play fetch. When he's hungry he eats some treats.

What is the name of the dog?

What is the name of the dog's owner?

What color is the dog?

What games does the dog play?

Name

Teacher

Class

Date

Shape Sorter

Jai needs help sorting his things between flat shapes and solid forms. Can you help him out? **Circle the 2D shapes and box the 3D forms.**

Name: ______________________ Date: ______________________

I can write my name

NAME: ______________________ DATE: ______________

SECTION: ______________________ SCORE: ______________

COUNTING ON THE FARM

Let's find out how many animals Farmer Ben has!

Directions: Count how many sheep, cows, horses, chickens, and goats Farmer Ben has. Write your answers in the boxes below. Then add how many animals he has altogether.

Sheep

Cows

Horses

Chickens

Horses

______________ ANIMALS

Name: .... Date: ....

Teacher: .... Class: ....

Find the words

Finish the sentences using the correct words below.

legs	round	months
chocolate	fur	year

A ball is ....

The table has four ....

My dog has white ....

The cake has .... frosting.

A year has twelve ....

I celebrate my birthday every ....

Name

Teacher

Class

Date

Find the missing number

Solve the equations below.

10 – 0 = ☐

5 – 4 = ☐

5 – 3 = ☐

2 – 0 = ☐

7 – 4 = ☐

4 – 1 = ☐

8 – 4 = ☐

1 – 0 = ☐

7 – 6 = ☐

5 – 1 = ☐

Name

Date

Section

Score

MEET MY HERO

ALL SET TO WRITE AN INFORMATIVE ESSAY?

Start by answering this question: Who is your hero? Give details about their background, qualities, and achievements. You can also mention why you look up to them.

Name:

Teacher:

Grade & Section:

Date:

Cathematics

Solve the following word problems.
Don't forget to share your solutions!

1.

Tamara has two cats. One of her cats gave birth to three kittens. How many cats does Tamara now have?

2.

The cat shelter has twelve cats. Dev adopted two of them. How many cats does the shelter have left?

3.

A cat followed Soojin home. She already has three cats. How many cats does she now have?

4.

Zander rescued six kittens. His best friend Darryl adopted two of them. How many kittens does Zander have left?

5.

Jada brought three of her cats to the vet. Her friend, Emily, brought two. How many cats did the girls bring together?

Name: ______________________ Teacher: ______________________

Class: ______________________ Date: ______________________

Active and Passive Voice

Underline the verb in the sentences below. Identify if the sentence is written in the active voice or the passive voice by checking the correct box. If the sentence is in the active voice, rewrite the sentence in the passive voice and vice versa. Write your revision on the corresponding blank.

1. April was writing a letter to her grandmother.

☐ Active Voice ☐ Passive Voice

____

2. Because of his many achievements, the actor will be honored at the ceremony.

☐ Active Voice ☐ Passive Voice

____

3. My notebook has been misplaced.

☐ Active Voice ☐ Passive Voice

____

4. They are building a robot that can play video games.

☐ Active Voice ☐ Passive Voice

____

5. This beautiful sculpture was created by one of our greatest living artists.

☐ Active Voice ☐ Passive Voice

____

Name

Teacher

Class

Date

MISSING DOTS

Complete the equation by drawing the missing dots.

+ = 10

+ = 5

+ = 8

+ = 7

+ = 4

+ = 6

+ = 3

+ = 8

+ = 2

+ = 9

ABOUT MY DAY

USE THESE SENTENCE STARTERS

NAME	SECTION
DATE	SCORE

COMPLETE ONE, TWO, OR ALL OF THESE LINES BELOW:

Today was a good/bad day for me because

I was excited to

I got the opportunity to

I didn't expect to

Name:

Class/Section:

Date:

Score:

Understanding Shapes

LET'S DRAW AND COLOR!

I. Color the squares blue, the circles red, and the triangles green.

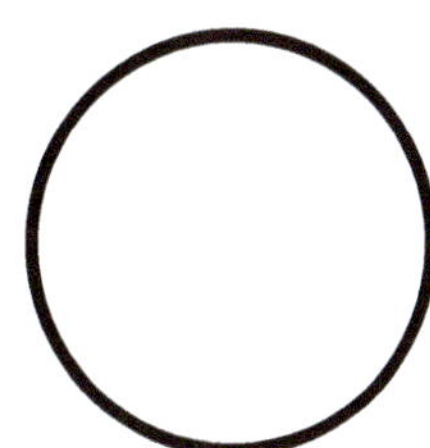

II. Draw two objects for each shape on the space provided below.

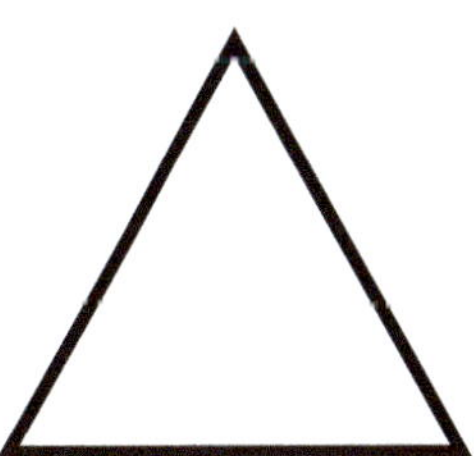

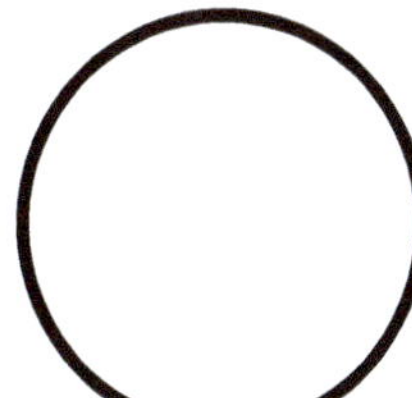

MY FIRST JOURNAL

All About Me!

NAME

SECTION

DATE

TEACHER

My favorite food is ... (explain in detail)

The Counting Game

Prepared By: ____________________

Name: ____________________ Section: ____________________

Date: ____________________ Score: ____________________

Instructions: Fill in the missing numbers as you count from 1 to 50.

1	2	3	___	5	6	7	8	9	___
11	12	___	14	___	16	17	18	___	20
21	___	___	___	___	___	27	28	29	30
___	32	___	___	35	___	___	___	39	40
___	42	___	44	___	46	47	48	49	50

RHYME TIME

Write words that rhyme with your spelling words.

Word	Rhyming Word
tree	knee, free, see

NAME: DATE:

SECTION: SCORE:

OH, LOOK AT THE TIME!

It's time for a little activity about angles.

Directions: Below are pictures of clocks with two hands that make one angle. Use your protractor to find out if they make an acute or obtuse angle. Remember to double check your answers before you submit your paper!

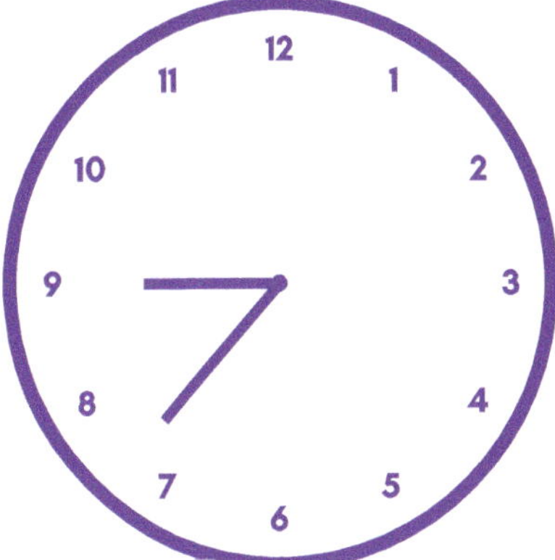

NAME

SECTION

DATE

TEACHER

Telling Stories

Write an 2-5 page story based on this prompt:

Two people are in the supermarket. They both try to grab the same item. Realizing it's the last one in stock, both of them need to figure out who gets it.

Name ____________________ Teacher ____________________

Class ____________________ Date ____________________

Time to do subtraction!

6 -3	7 -5	10 -3	8 -2
8 -7	6 -1	3 -2	5 -2
7 -3	10 -5	8 -1	7 -7
5 -2	9 -4	8 -3	9 -3

Name:

Date:

You Can Be Anything!

Bessie Coleman wanted to be a pilot at a time when it was difficult for a woman and a Black person to do so. With her hard work and persistence, she overcame her challenges and reached her goal.

What do you want to be? Draw it in the space below.

What are the things you can do to help you reach your goal?

Write down the words that might block what you want to do... then cross them out!

COLOR BY SHAPE

CAN YOU SEE THE HIDDEN SHAPES?

Name:

Section:

Date:

Score:

Find the shapes in the picture and color them in based on the guide below.

Triangles = Red
Squares = Yellow
Rectangles = Blue
Rhombus = Green
Circles = Orange
Ovals = Purple

Name:

Date:

Section:

Score:

Opposite words

Draw a line to match the word on the left to its opposite.

wet	slow
hot	many
long	hard
fast	dry
dark	bright
soft	short
smooth	old
young	rough
few	cold

Fishy Mathematics

Let's learn the Equal, Less & Greater Than Symbols

Name:

Date:

Section:

Score:

Count the fish in the fishbowls and write down the correct number. Then, compare the number and write > , < or = to show which fishbowl has more, less, or equal number of fish.

1. ☐  ___  ☐

2. ☐  ___  ☐

3. ☐  ___  ☐

Name:

Class:

Date:

Score:

This Week's Sentence Starters

Write a short essay using this sentence starter:

If I could be another person for a day,
I want to be _____.

Name: ______________

Section: ______________

____

Date: ______________

Score: ______________

____

SNAKE PARTY

Figure out how many snakes are in the party!

There are several snakes all tangled up in this snake party! Use your coloring materials to distinguish how many snakes there are in total!

TOTAL

Name: ______________________ Teacher: ______________

Grade & Section: ______________________ Date: ______________

LET'S COLOR LETTERS

Color the uppercase letters red.

Color the lowercase letters blue.

Name:

Date:

Section:

Score:

Candy Store

How many candies does Jane get?

Jane is in a candy store and has three gold coins. She wants to get some strawberry bonbons! Three strawberry bonbons cost one gold coin. How much strawberry bonbons can Jane get with her three gold coins? Multiply and write your answer on the space below:

NAME:

DATE:

Mood Match

Can you tell the color of the feelings below? Color the word box of each picture based on the mood thermometer.

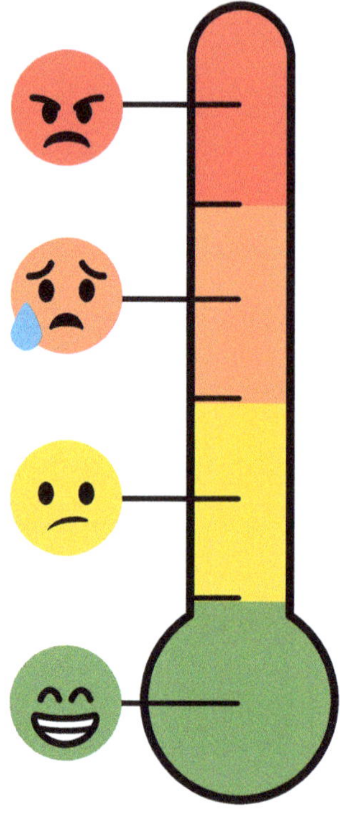

happy

sad

hurt

shy

loved

tired

silly

scared

Mrs. Green's Fruit Stand

Name:

Teacher:

Grade & Section:

Date:

Mrs. Green sells fruit in boxes of 8.
Make sure each box has eight by drawing the missing fruit.

Name:

Date:

Things we see in school

Trace the words then write them in the space next to it.

SAM SELLS SEASHELLS

Name: ____________________ Section: ____________________

Date: ____________________ Score: ____________________

COUNT HOW MANY SEASHELLS ARE SOLD BY THE SEASHORE.

Directions: Add the numbers found in the two small seashells then jot down the answer on the big seashell. Be the first to submit your paper with all the correct answers to win a prize!

10 + 13 =

7 + 18 =

4 + 8 =

5 + 11 =

Rhyming Words

NAME:

TEACHER:

CLASS:

DATE:

Circle the word that rhymes with the word inside the box.

cat	bat	clap
pan	saw	can
bee	see	me
hand	land	bend
mop	lap	cop
lip	skip	drip

LET'S PRACTICE ROUNDING UP!

Paul needs to prepare his payment at the supermarket. Round up the prices of the following items, so Paul can pay and get his change:

Item	Price	Rounded
1 box of toothpaste	$2.10	$
1 bag of apples	$5.15	$
1 bag of chips	$3.50	$
1 bottle of orange juice	$5.35	$
1 carton of milk	$3.25	$

Name: ______________________ Section: ______________________

Date: ______________________ Score: ______________________

Identify the picture

Color the box with the correct object name.

lunch box

pen case

mirror

glasses

paper

book

scissors

ruler

car

house

banana

apple

key

ring

pencil

eraser

NAME: ______________________ TEACHER: ______________________

GRADE & SECTION: ______________________ DATE: ______________________

LONG, LONGER, LONGEST

Which one is it? Number the following groups with 1, 2, and 3 to show which one is long, longer, and longest.

Name

Teacher

Class

Date

Find the Same Letters

Draw a circle around all the letter K's you see.

k r K A R z o S m b

K n L N C k T k E n S

a R K A z H r j n q

N d L S N k T k i n U

c K o E N X f w b u G

The Ice Cream Factory

Learning about numbers!

NAME

SECTION

SCORE

DATE

Mr. Anders needs your help to create the perfect ice cream.
Read the instructions and use crayons to draw your answer.

DRAW 2 SCOOPS OF CHOCOLATE	DRAW 3 SCOOPS OF STRAWBERRY	DRAW 4 SCOOPS OF BLUEBERRY

Name: ______________________ Date: ______________________

Matching Easter Eggs

Draw a line to match the easter eggs that look the same. Then, color all the eggs.

Name: ____________ Date: ____________

Skip Counting

Count in 5's to find the total.

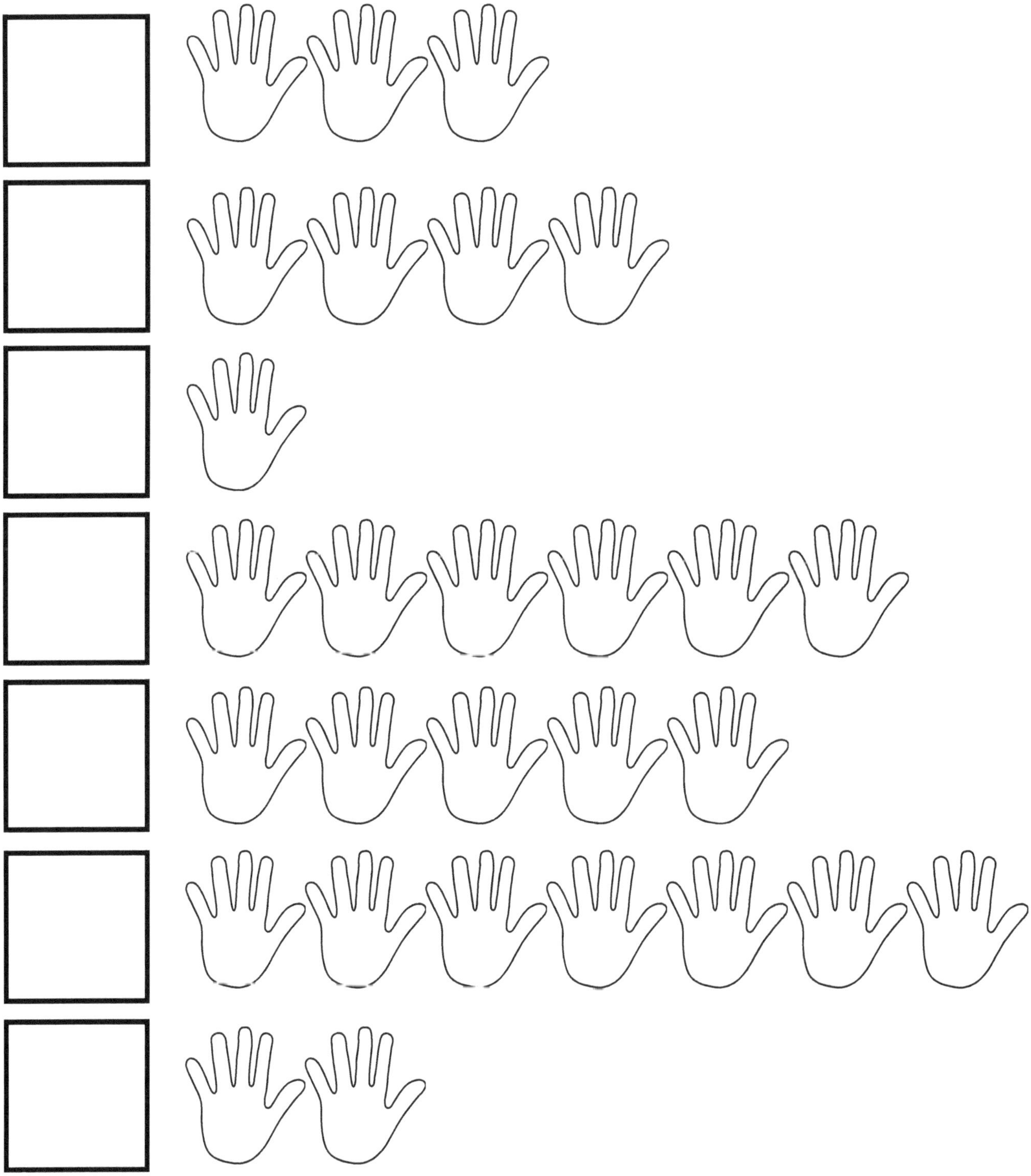

Name: ____________________ Teacher: ____________________

Grade & Section: ____________________ Date: ____________________

WHO AM I?

Use the space below to draw a self-portrait. On the left side, draw how you look on the outside. On the right side, draw your favorite toys, animals, food, or games. Color your creation when you're done!

Materials: Pencil, Paper, Crayons

NAME DATE

CLASS SCORE

ROCKET MATH

Solve the equations to launch the rockets!

Prints and Patterns

Using the different materials you brought, create a unique pattern for each of the unicorns below. Combine geometric and organic shapes to make your patterns.

Subject: Art

Materials: Paper, Pencil, Poster Paint, Watercolor, Paintbrushes, Oil Pastels, Markers, Crayons, and Colored Pencils

Name: ____________________ Teacher: ____________________

Grade & Section: ____________________ Date: ____________________

Name:	Section:
Date:	Teacher:

Number Values

Color the number that has the bigger value

5 8	4 5
6 0	3 2
9 5	4 7
8 2	6 1

Name:

Section:

Teacher:

Date:

SUMMER WORD SEARCH

Look for the words listed below.

S	U	N	W	A	N	P	U	A
U	S	B	A	E	I	P	L	H
N	H	T	T	W	C	L	S	O
B	E	N	E	U	E	A	A	T
L	L	W	R	R	D	Y	N	N
O	L	N	B	O	T	S	D	F
C	A	M	B	E	A	C	H	U
K	U	W	A	V	E	S	C	N
P	I	N	E	A	P	P	L	E

Sun	Waves	Fun	Pineapple
Sunblock	Hot	Beach	Water
Play	Sand	Shell	Umbrella

Name

Class

Teacher

Date

Greater or Less than

Compare the numbers and write <, >, or =

10 ◯ 8	1 ◯ 10
6 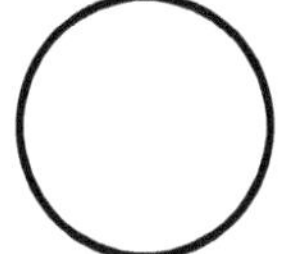 7	3  3
5 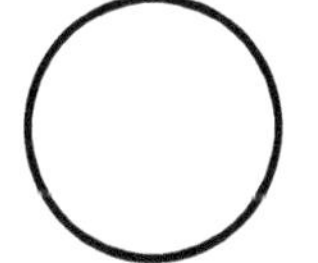 5	0  8
3 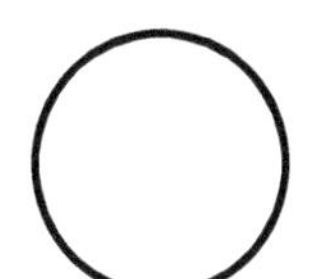 9	7 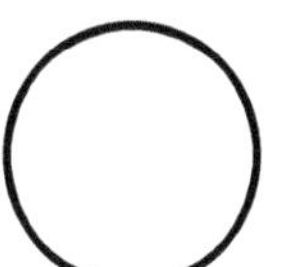 9
4 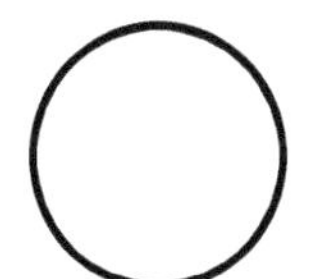 2	6 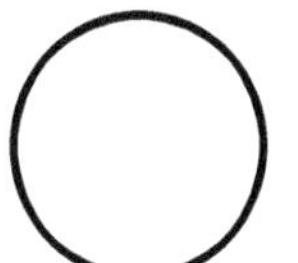 4

NAME: ______________________ TEACHER: ______________________

GRADE & SECTION: ______________________ DATE: ______________________

THE FOOD WEB

Animals in an ecosystem form a food web. In the illustration below, use arrows to map out the energy transfer between organisms. The first one has been added as an example.

Name two producers in the food web above.

____

____

____

Name three consumers in the food web above.

____

____

____

What is the difference between food chains and food webs?

____

____

____

Name: __________ Section: __________ Date: __________ Score: __________

Match The Shapes

Draw a line from the object on the left to the shape that matches it.

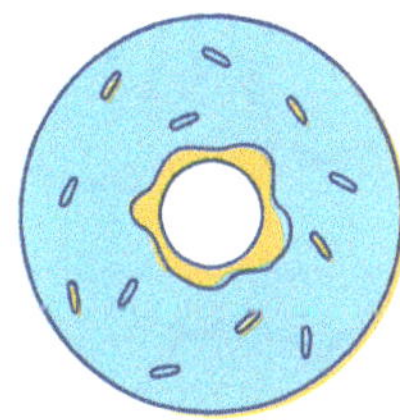

Name: .... Date: ....

HELLO, SPRING!

Let's color these flowers and butterflies to welcome the Spring season.

DID YOU KNOW?

In Spring, flowers grow faster and bloom. That's because plants react to temperature and light during this season. Higher temperatures and longer days affect the growth and flowering of many plant species.

Source: "8 Facts about Spring." Paraligo.com , 20 Mar. 2015, paraligo.com/en/did-you-know/8-facts-about-spring/.

SOLAR SYSTEM CROSSWORD

Answer the questions and fill in the crossword with the correct answers.

1. One turn around the Earth's axis every 24 hours is called ....
2. What is the center of our solar system?
3. This planet is famous for its red spot.

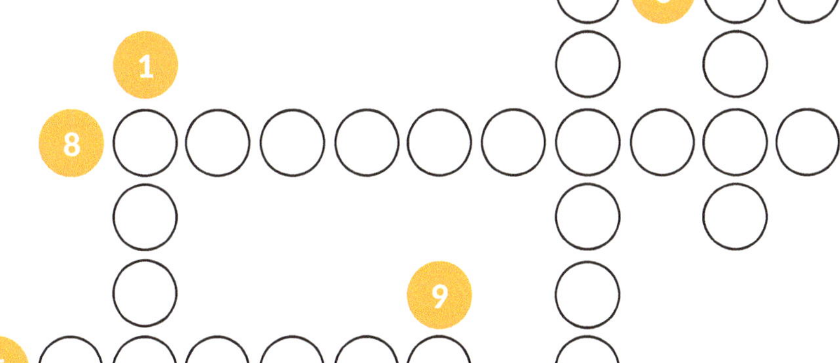

4. Which planet has the most number of rings?
5. What objects are commonly made of snow, ice, and dust, and can be found moving around outer space?
6. Which planet has the moons Phobos and Deimos?
7. This is Earth's satellite.
8. The moon's light is caused by .... from the Earth.
9. The Sun is a ....
10. This occurs when one heavenly body (moon or planet) moves into the shadow of another.

Name ______________ Grade ______________

Date ______________ Teacher ______________

Name:

Class:

Date:

Score:

Fun with Fractions

LEARN HOW TO ADD AND SUBTRACT FRACTIONS!

Write down the fraction indicated by each drawing in each row then write down the answer to the problem.

www.ingramcontent.com/pod-product-compliance
Ingram Content Group UK Ltd.
Pitfield, Milton Keynes, MK11 3LW, UK
UKHW050142280726
14058UKWH00006B/792